RATIONAL ANTHEM

Miller Williams Poetry Series
EDITED BY PATRICIA SMITH

RATIONAL ANTHEM

Casey Thayer

The University of Arkansas Press
Fayetteville
2022

ISBN: 978-1-68226-204-7
eISBN: 978-1-61075-773-7

26 25 24 23 22   5 4 3 2 1

Manufactured in the United States of America

Designed by Liz Lester

∞ The paper used in this publication meets the minimum requirements of the American National Standard for Permanence of Paper for Printed Library Materials Z39.48-1984.

Library of Congress Cataloging-in-Publication Data
Names: Thayer, Casey, 1983– author.
Title: Rational anthem / Casey Thayer.
Description: Fayetteville: University of Arkansas Press, 2022. | Series: Miller Williams poetry prize | Summary: "Casey Thayer's Rational Anthem offers wry tribute to 'the greatest country God could craft with the mules he had / on hand.' In seeking to tell the story of the ragged world around him, Thayer examines the links among flag-waving populism, religious fervor, and toxic masculinity"—Provided by publisher.
Identifiers: LCCN 2021050708 (print) | LCCN 2021050709 (ebook) | ISBN 9781682262047 (paperback) | ISBN 9781610757737 (ebook)
Subjects: LCGFT: Poetry.
Classification: LCC PS3620.H383 R38 2022 (print) | LCC PS3620.H383 (ebook) | DDC 811/.6—dc23
LC record available at https://lccn.loc.gov/2021050708
LC ebook record available at https://lccn.loc.gov/2021050709

for Jacques

CONTENTS

I believe that all of us, every poet everywhere, can point to one mortifying moment of clueless ambition, when we decided that it was a snazzy idea to skip several thousand steps in our poetic evolution. After all, we were the annoying kids who bragged that we could and would memorize the entire dictionary, one page a day. (I threw in the towel at *abattoir*. You?)

Undeterred by the failure to master the all of our language, I once again succumbed to an unbridled zeal. Once I chose poetry as my way to walk through the world, and anxious to get down to business, I decided that I'd teach myself prosody and form in one big ol' fell swoop. Who needed classrooms and seminars and actual instruction? I'd picked up the enticing tome *Patterns of Poetry*, by some guy named Miller Williams, in the best lil' bookstore in Chicago, and I'd set aside a whole month to memorize everything in its pages.

Imagine—an entire *month* to master iambs, dactyls, anapests, pyrrhus, spondees, trochees and amphibrachs, as well as sapphics, the elegiac couplet, englyn penfyr, dipodic quatrain, awdyl gywydd, clerihew, terza rima, cyhydedd hir, rhupunt, and—well, the sonnet, of course.

This Williams person, whoever he was (remember that I was— shall we say, oblivious to everything except my own naked desire to POET), had gathered all that juicy knowledge between two covers, and all I had to do was sit down and pick it up. I imagined him on a misty mountainside somewhere, wallowing in wisdom and doling out prosody. I'd soon be joining him.

Needless to say, failure was my one and only option. It is notoriously difficult to teach yourself metrics because so much depends on hearing it from someone who's got it mastered and internalized. As Annie Finch—the woman who eventually got poetic rhythms through my thick skull—said, "If you never feel it in your body, you'll never feel it."

It is also notoriously difficult to teach the emotional and narrative nuances of form. A poet has a dizzying amount of power when it comes to topic, perspective, and voice, and even more power when it comes to choosing the form that will pull it all together. As I like to tell my students, every single choice you make as a poet instructs the reader in the reading of the poem. EVERY. SINGLE. CHOICE.

In the midst of tackling *Patterns of Poetry* and failing miserably at both the patterns and the poetry, I thought I'd take some time to get to know more about that Williams fella. Whenever he used his own poems as examples in the book, I was tempted to throw the volume across the room into the nearest wall—they were that good.

I still crave the gorgeously stuttered music of the elegiac couplets in "For Victor Jara":

This is to say we remember. Not that remembering saves us.
Not that remembering brings anything usable back.

This is to say that we never have understood how to say this.
Out of our long unbelief what do we say to belief?

And this, my favorite excerpt from "On the Way Home from Nowhere, New Year's Eve":

I tell myself I am blind. In such a dark
I could be moving down the spaceless form
of time, a painted tunnel. I twist off
my shoes and walk in darkness. Leap.

Soon I realized that the idea of book learnin' myself into poetic prowess was a hopeless undertaking. But instead of giving up altogether, I decided to do a deep dive into Mr. Williams's work. I learned for the first time that he'd been William Jefferson Clinton's inaugural poet ("Whose law was never so much of the hand as the head / cannot let chaos make its way to the heart . . ."). I scoured the *Poetry* magazine archives, where this stanza of "For Rebecca, for Whom Nothing Has Been Written Page after Page" waited for me:

When all the words are written down and read
and even the creeping weights are written in
what matters is what remains not said, not said.
Which is what long silences are for.

And in his book *The Ways We Touch*, I found the wee treasure "Compassion," which urges its reader to shower each and everyone with empathy "even if they don't want it"—because—

> You do not know what wars are going on
> down there where the spirit meets the bone.

Well, amen.

After throwing his books against the wall in frustration, what drew me deeper into Miller Williams's work? The same thing that should draw me to yours.

I look for new ways to look at things I've already seen—things I'm convinced I know. I look for a hook for my breath to catch on. I look for form—traditional that enhances, instead of suffocates, its subject matter. Williams makes me jealous. He makes me wish I'd written it first.

And according to the man himself: "One of the best things that has ever been said about my work was said by a critic who wrote that 'Miller Williams is the Hank Williams of American poetry. While his poetry is taught at Princeton and Harvard, it's read and understood by squirrel hunters and taxi drivers.'"

In other words, I'm addicted to poetry that knows no closed doors.

It's been years between the time I first reveled in the words of this newfound poet and the day I became the editor of this series that carries his name. But both nothing much and everything has changed. I still need and expect to be knocked to the floor by a poem. I need it to hold me down, make me breathe differently. I'm a selfish reader. I want everything from a poem—and I know, for a fact, that everything isn't too much. *I want poems that vivify.*

You may, at this very moment, be thinking about submitting your lovingly spit-shined manuscript to the contest. If so, I have some pointers. (First of all, don't spit on it.)

My stellar contest screeners are also my teachers—I see in their work that they are dead set on narrative and lyrical impact, so I'm certain that the poems they read and forwarded to me have reached for that dual goal and achieved it.

But they also saw many manuscripts that weren't quite ready for the big time—by poets I like to think of as "feverishly pulling the trigger, but lacking ammunition"—or manuscripts that were enthusiastically submitted to exactly the wrong contest. The directive is, and always will be, very very simple: Read the description of what we want. Then send your one-of-a-kind, patented version of *that*.

In my college classrooms, officially "grading" poetry has always struck me as a bit of a crapshoot, because students enter at so many different levels with so many different ideas of what poetry is. I once had a fledgling writer pen a textured and lyrically complicated persona poem in the voice of a chambered bullet. In the very same class, a lovelorn student wrote, "When you left me, you hurt my emotions."

But the manuscripts that poured into the Miller Williams contest, for the most part, had obviously been sweated, prayed, and wept over, revised to pinpoint, whipped into formidable shape. There was a universal goodness to the mix, even if not everyone paid close enough attention to the type of work requested. But, oh—the top three certainly did. Each, in their own way, rocked the rafters.

Once J. Bailey Hutchinson's *Gut* rocketed to the top of the pile, it pretty much stayed there. Yes, there were contenders who threatened the throne, but *Gut* was always strolling in the neighborhood of the kingdom. It's startling and innovative and—how shall I say this?—a little bit of everyone. You'll see yourself here somewhere.

I really wish I'd written it.

But making sure it reaches you is definitely the next best thing.

Listen to this. It's the closing lines of "Ouroboros as Eight-Year-Old," one of the poems in the book about Bailey growing up with ADHD:

> she leans down to kiss the top of my head and I leap, I put her teeth through her lip. And. She holds. My mother's arms come around me. Even as I boil. Even as I pulse. Even as *spilled swim-bladder which is accumulated dollop of sap which is liquid which sticks which is inside an eel-bird inside a gas giant* which is blood on my scalp, which is my mother's exploded mouth, teeth two pearls in a red bed, *which is deconstructed willow-weeper which is a nest of purpled popsicle sticks*, she holds. Even as I become a jar of furious bones.

She holds. My head a walnut in the quiet vise of her chin. Swollen grape in a lionsmouth.

There you have it. One of the many hooks I caught my breath on. The sound. The surprise. The collision of phrases I thought could never collide. The current of love and trust flowing beneath it all.

What stands out about Bailey's work is her singular voice, graced with the ease and imagination of a born storyteller. She's a southern girl who sees no need to pound in that fact with a narrative hammer. She simply lifts you up and places you in the dead center of an addictive poetic lifeline, populated by cinema-worthy backdrops and people who refuse to stop nudging once you're done with the book.

The unforgiving edges of the poet's grandmother, Barbara, that "mean / sleepwalking woman" whose ghost "comes up from the river,   drenched in coontail kelp and fresh-mussel, // pale   as a goat throat."

Bailey's mother Mitzi, she of the wise and halting wisdoms, steps alive in the multisectioned "Became My Body, Too," stanzas of fractured and loving lineage. Here, a young Mitzi watches for her sister's seizures.

> At night, Mitzi would kneel by her sister's bunk
> with a garden-trowel   the grip all gnawed,
> (*how can a mouth   so small   blister*
>   *beechwood?*)—watching
> for the pulse of jaw,   the frenetic socket-whirl
> that took the girl's body
> before she became crack of cymbal   and seafloor
>   lightning.

And her granddaddy Hoyle—his ways with women and meat, his hard ways of loving—will be with you for a long, long time. This, from "The Butcher's Granddaughter":

> This body. Its rope. Before some pea-ball burst
> his brain, I remember Hoyle's belly—me, curled
> like a grub there, grogged on applesauce. He smelled
> like a good lunch meat, the biggest man I knew, singing
> *too-ra-loo-ra-lai* through a mouth I never heard bite.

In addition, Bailey has mastered something I look for that not many poets can accomplish, something I'm constantly trying to get better at—when there's something she wants the reader to feel and there's no exact word for it, she conjures a phrase: Beer "nickeling my brain's-edge." A man is "shirt-wrecked by a midnight nosebleed." "Screwed to a scaffold, body-water glossy, / the hog opens like a Bible." A postcard is crammed with "cricket-leg lettering."

J. Bailey Hutchinson keeps introducing me and introducing me and introducing me to more and more brand-new world. Nothing settles. Nothing sits still. Nothing "makes do."

Thanks to this utterly original voice, my very first series pick is everything I was looking for.

Meanwhile, Janet Jackson (how's that for a segue?), who I go to for all my pithy wisdom, once said of her famously gruff father, "My dad taught us that there's no greater distance than that between first and second place."

That most definitely applies if you're a Jackson, but not in the case of Casey Thayer and his amazing second-place manuscript *Rational Anthem*.

It's hard to find a way to say this without someone taking offense, but *Rational Anthem* is a stellar *boy* book, pulsing with the triumphs and downfalls of testosterone, a muscled book, a book that's decidedly cocked and loaded. It's a book of men who drag their feet through violence. It's a painstakingly scrawled love letter to firepower. It chronicles men in their struggles with tenderness and vulnerability. It's the hunter and the blood and gristle the hunter knows. It's a book that not many people—certainly not many men, tangled in the roots of everything they think they should be—could write with such revelation and nuance.

Consider this, from "An Anatomical Study Concerning the North American Whitetail":

You can love a man and find some shared action
in which he tolerates that love.

I slid my hands up the hollow muffler
of the buck's chest cavity

and slit the esophagus, cut the skirt
of the diaphragm from sternum to crotch.

Then I pulled the guts out. Sometimes
I believe in small acts of kindness.

Rational Anthem often finds itself at the juncture of what a man
does and what he dares to feel, and for the reader that's traditionally
a shadowy and unknowable place. But Casey fearlessly inhabits that
space, moving in the lens until we move from discomfort to discovery:

> **bullet • 1.** what thunder, teeth / in the threat, / blade in the
> sheath, / blood-letter bought / over the counter as easy as
> aspirin or an Oxy / to take into the body, / what the deed /
> leaves, hand that reaches / across the field, / snake coiled in
> the warren, / mole mazing the loam, / what the body carries,
> what is left / of the deed . . .

I certainly don't mean to imply that *Rational Anthem* is *all* boy.
There is much notable otherwise in its pages, including an unsettling
ars poetica, an unstructured abecedarian that hits like a backhand
slap, and cameos by Aquaman and an adopted blue whale.

But what *Rational Anthem* offers is crucial insight on how men
think when they can't help but think. As the opening stanza of "The
next great American elegy in the effigy of" indicates, the book is a
deep dive into that riddle:

> you, who bonged from a severed boar's head
> Yuengling poured down its throat into your throat,
> who let the jaws of that giant clamp yours in a kiss,
> you, feral and triumphant in owning an animal for sport.

Casey Thayer's fearless exploration of masculinity is nothing less
than revelatory. It manages to be contemplative and insightful, while
packing a relentless punch. I will surely be gifting it to a few manly
types who I hope will benefit from its bravery.

Since Janet Jackson never blurted any wisdoms about *third* place
(my guess is that, for her father, no such thing existed), I won't be
quoting her again in my introduction of Michael Mlekoday's *All
Earthly Bodies.*

While Bailey and Casey do their vivifying head-on, with narratives that unfurl like cinema, Michael's punch is quieter—but its more gradual force, wrapped in a muscled language, still whips your head around. I loud-whispered "damn!" so often while reading this manuscript, my husband—the crime-writing poetry snob—barged into my office to see what was doing such a number on my head.

So I read him the opening lines of "Revolting":

> Even the gaze
> is a kind of government
>
> and even the outlaw
> wants sometimes
> to kneel
>
> if only in a field
> as full as a revolver.

And, just like that, he understood.

After the names of the winner and runners-up were initially revealed, I looked into their backgrounds. I was surprised and delighted to discover that Michael had been a regular participant in the poetry slam, the often-controversial competition where head-on vivifying is pretty much the order of the day.

The slam, aside from being a sometimes-chaotic performative arena, was also an invaluable training ground for the development of physical and social witnessing that brought *All Earthly Bodies* to this moment. In a perfect world, this is what the slammer becomes—a poet at the crosswords of resistance and rhythm, someone who knows that poetry's power resides not only in the scream, but often in the whisper.

Listen to this excerpt from the heart-numbing "The Night the Murderous Cop Was Not Charged":

> I want to know where
> all this weeping and standing
> has taken us, exactly. [. . .]

Does the infinite static
of the Pacific's evening tide—
everbearing, acidifying—
flicker itself to justice?

Can the long memories
of the pines imagine
something like restitution
for all the blades, blights,

and wildfires we call
history?

And it is Michael who penned that snippet I printed out and pinned above my desk. There's always that passage that steps gingerly from the manuscript to shake you into a new awake. Here it is, from "Whites":

But what is quotation exactly,
if not a way to wield another's prayer
and pretend it is not our own.

What language is not borrowed
machinery, echo of another's ancestors
burrowing the whole field of you,

blooming a grain you can't name
but harvest regardless.

—Patricia Smith

ACKNOWLEDGMENTS

Grateful acknowledgment is made to the editors of the following journals in which these poems, sometimes in earlier versions or under different titles, first appeared: *Adroit Journal*: "Blood Work"; *AGNI*: "An Anatomical Study Concerning the North American Whitetail"; *American Poetry Review*: "Book of Grudges," "Drowning doesn't look like drowning," "The next great American elegy in the effigy of," and "Rational Anthem"; *Devil's Lake*: "Our Congregation of the World Weary" and "The Problem with Poetry"; *Florida Review*: "After Dark"; *Linebreak*: "Aquaman Thinks of His Youth"; *Memorious: A Journal of New Verse and Fiction*: "My Quarry"; *Poetry*: "The Hurt Sonnet"; *Prairie Schooner*: "Lifeguard" and "My God"; *RHINO*: "For Dennis, the Blue Whale I Adopted in Grade School" and "Randy Be Drowning"; *Southern Indiana Review*: "Hymn for the Colt"; *Vinyl Poetry*: "Black String of Days," "[bullet • 1.]," and "[trigger • 1.]"; and *ZYZZYVA*: "Play."

Some of these poems appear in *Love for the Gun*, a chapbook selected by Marcus Wicker as winner of the 2020 Cow Creek Chapbook Prize sponsored by Pittsburg State University.

This book would not have been possible without the support of the Sewanee Writers' Conference and Sidney Wade, and the Creative Writing Program at Stanford University and the mentorship extended by its faculty and its Jones and Stegner fellows, especially Eavan Boland, W. S. Di Piero, Kenneth Fields, Louise Glück, Austin Smith, Brian Tierney, and Corey Van Landingham. Thank you to Kai Carlson-Wee, Ben Jackson, Nate Klug, Cate Lycurgus, Silvia Oviedo López, Eric Raymond, and the rest of the PT SF crew for a creative life raft during the pandemic. Thank you to Tara Ebrahimi, Ann Hudson, Matthew Kelsey, Lindsay Garbutt, Michael Garza, Willie James, Faisal Mohyuddin, Jacob Saenz, and the rest of the PT CHI crew for the pressure of deadlines. Thank you to Jacques Rancourt for your unfailing friendship.

Thank you to Patricia Smith for selecting this manuscript and to

David Scott Cunningham and everyone at the University of Arkansas Press, especially Janet Foxman, for making it a reality.

Most of all, thank you to Stella, who teaches me how to patiently wait for what I want; Frances, who amazes me with her curiosity, energy, and goofiness; and Leslie, who shows me the true definition of commitment and support. I've enjoyed too much luck having you three in my life to ask for more.

trigger • 1. a liberator, pulls / the pin on what you've hidden—
caution: / this content can upset, what's inside you, / how it
explodes in moments / of weakness, being / every day amazed by /
the willingness of strangers / to meet with grace this bare expression
of weakness, / the squat nub, half-moon apostrophe, / what's
second-thought / but not—the trigger's insistent, / to talk about it,
the need / to talk about it, / what to label, what to leave unlabeled,
/ to erase the mind & survive that erasure, / ringing in the ear, the
blood in the ear, / to teach yourself / to embrace what sets / off,
to hold it in your mouth / like a matchstick swallowed / by the
flame, or a landmine that means / to negate itself through its loud
& insistent protest, this test, / this testament / to life beyond the
body: / that to have a trigger makes you / a weapon.

RATIONAL ANTHEM

What haven't we pledged to the cause, suffered for our neighbor
in this, the greatest country God could craft with the mules he had

on hand—our Muppet Babies, our baby boomers, our baby soldiers,
our Hit Me Babies One More Time, our babies made of the ribs

of other babies. Let us sing, all you people, let us sing together
pop songs, join the unending hymn of Timberlake, genesis

of boy band fury, the resurrection of the sexy and the life
of the world to come. We'll have you know, our babies

got backs, got legs, got tiny hearts. Our babies have high
infant mortality rates. What haven't we pledged

to ourselves in the thirtieth second of a legendary
keg stand as those around us chant "we will, we will

rock you," since the Lord sees fit to rock us on a school night?
Beatbox us. Binge drink us. We've been driven mad

by the best minds of our generation. What haven't we
promised to our country late at night to get a piece of ass?

America, we'll care enough to kill for you, we'll spread your legs
and fill the empty space. America, that bitch is crazy.

We never had sex with that woman. For this game,
you'll need a partner, a pair of dice, and a blatant disregard

for risk. For this game, you'll need to bundle all your assets
into one account. The world will know it's on

when we bring out chips, set up the poker table, and purchase
party favors. This is our house. It's a very very very

fine house. We're the bait and switch, the set-up.
We're ringers waiting for our turn to win.

America, let me keep you to have and to hold.
I'll poke holes in your lid. I'll give you mouth-to-mouth.

Our declaration included wide-eyed wonderment and relief
that a country could wrap us up like a present. Our preamble

gave us one nation, wracked with debt and credit collectors,
one holy static and ecstatic talk show host and a healthy dose

of media coverage. The point is, America, you are the shit,
you are the life of the party, you are the most flattering light.

So to your fluorescence, your love light halogen over us.
Let it shine. Don't put it under a bushel. Let it shine.

PLAY

Our goal: to claim the best
six-shooter or shotgun

rooted from windthrow or snapped
from lower branches.

After battle, my father broke
them down for the burn pile,

but each morning the forest
filled with weapons.

They were so easy to find.
If we shot a boy, he had to

admit he died. This all rested
on mutual agreement.

Sometimes
we beat the boy with switches

because he wouldn't die,
though we agreed he had.

KEYS OF THE RED MAPLE

Da Vinci never traveled to America,
but I want to imagine what sparked
his idea for the helicopter
was an afternoon he spent
under a red maple in late September
on the banks of Lake Michigan
as it shed from its branches
the blades of its samaras.
They would have winged down
to land in dune grass and the cracks
between the slats of his Adirondack.
The simplicity in the design.
Keys caught in the coarse curls
of his beard, snagged in his hose,
so if he rose, he'd carry a few
with him back to Florence.
The banks of Lake Michigan.
A maple with birds in the boughs.
On a sunny afternoon in September
that didn't happen, I want
to imagine him sitting there,
inventing a new way for us to fly,
to take tourists past a volcano's
dormant yet smoking cone, to hover
above Thursday's rush-hour
interstate delays, but mainly
to service finance bros escaping
the city for tee times and cocktails
at the nineteenth hole.

The coupled wings of samaras
offer a comparison so apparent,
it's pat, how they spiral,
how the lake breeze catches
the blades, ribbed like the margins
of a moth's forewings.
From the novella about the boys
burning down an island: *The greatest
ideas are the simplest.* Nobel stumbled
upon dynamite by accident,
noticing the porous rock
soaking up the nitroglycerin,
which made it stable, which allowed
its transportation. Hoping to front
an invasion of trees, the achenes
are designed for colonizing,
to spread offspring far from
the parent. In my reading,
I learn the helicopter entered
America's collective memory
perched on the rooftop
of an apartment complex
in Saigon as evacuees crowded
a ladder, attempting the summit,
the runways occupied or lost.
Apache, Black Hawk, Chinook
go by the shorthand *bird.*
All our ideas release from us.

Monarchs lifting from a maple's
crown as orange tracers.
Da Vinci never traveled these banks,
wedged his feet in the fine grit
of these beaches, but he drew
a map of the world that records
an early use of the name *America*,
stuck like a bull in the center.
What a discovery.

HYMN FOR THE COLT

Weighing a casing in my hand, I learned to love
the gun, my protector. Or my captor.

My father gifting it to me, all that
thunder, all that makes a man a man

to fear, a judge, an arbiter of justice.
Said my father: not like that. Here's how

you hold it. With every shot I closed
my eyes and after kept it always

unloaded—never loved enough
the power he claimed it gave.

Said the horse trainer: it's not
the rough stuff that works. So I worked

at growing softer, held the halter
like a hurt bird, perhaps a swallow.

Not like my father, as a man might do:
with a firm grip. From the Czech "to whistle,"

a pistol could be a burner, hole punch, Miss
Spray 'N Pray. It could be a heater, hip-rider,

holster tied around a thigh. Or gat,
slug chucker, nine. But I felt closer to colts

than the ropes the summer I saddle-broke
horses to carve out a kitty. The trainer:

don't think it breaking but acclimating.
I weighed a casing in my hand and waited.

bullet • **1.** what thunder, teeth / in the threat, / blade in the sheath, / blood-letter bought / over the counter as easy as aspirin or an Oxy / to take into the body, / what the deed / leaves, hand that reaches / across the field, / snake coiled in the warren, / mole mazing the loam, / what the body carries, what is left / of the deed, / shot from a muzzle, the muscle, / the missing piece but also the puzzle, / what measures a half-beat, / the period, the blow, / not immediate but in escrow, / death's long note guiding us / to sleep.

AN ANATOMICAL STUDY CONCERNING THE NORTH AMERICAN WHITETAIL

You can love a man and find some shared action
in which he tolerates that love.

I slid my hands up the hollow muffler
of the buck's chest cavity

and slit the esophagus, cut the skirt
of the diaphragm from sternum to crotch.

Then I pulled the guts out. Sometimes
I believe in small acts of kindness.

Sometimes I carry the heart in a plastic
Wonder Bread bag, shooing away a hound dog

who always has her ass against me on the couch,
in bed. I guess the cause is the comfort

of having her ass against something. I get it—
intimacy requires touch—so I carried the heart

and lungs, which we had a mind to pickle.
My father wiped the blade flat on his blaze,

lines of red on the orange the deer see as gray
and a slightly lighter shade of gray.

Someone tied the testicles to the trailer hitch.
I helped my father clean his hands with field grass,

convinced we had shared a moment
in rolling the internal organs out of the abdomen.

If you hold a heart, you can touch him.
He'll forget he's touching what he can't touch.

MY GOD

My god built a machine that builds machines—
he's a job creator. If your god's great,
mine's greater, not the jailer, but the jail,
not the lawyer, but the law incarnate,
jaws deep in the viscera, he caught
like Frankenstein's monster, a charge—
electric. My god gave birth to your god—
obstetrics. Scarecrow with a tummy full
of crows, shotgun a whitetail cuddles to
as the hunter nearly snores himself awake.
And there is the hiding of his power.
My god trades in any number of unregulated
American dialects: Yooper, Gulf Southern,
Emoji, Autocorrect. He twitpic his prick,
and it trended as *#That'sIt?* Small gods
make small promises, and who wants
to heat the whole house anyway?
My god plows or, all alone, he beats.
And every meal needs Wagyu beef.
My god's a scarecrow with a gut too big
to see his pecker, still he comes
correct—good grammar. His music
hits you so hard—MC Hammer.
Threat level green, belly full of Henny,
if my god speaks, men kill in his name,
lay blame in the multitudinous chorus.
· If you resist or flee, my god refuses
the rule to never fire at an animal's back—

if it's brown, it's down—and when you
complain about it, you displease my god
and my god hears it and my god
accounts for it. The earth quakes.
The foundations of the mountains tremble
with the echo of my god, my god, my god

IT'S FULL OF STARS

The mothers warned of bacteria
lurking in the AstroTurf, any skid

could grid our skin with doorways in.
I feared falling to the ground

from a hard tackle, carefully picked
my way through. Gun-shy, slow,

bent-waisted after crashing goal,
they sat me for the semis, but I

didn't care as long as I could claim
a screen-printed royal blue jersey.

To stand out would demand of me
a recklessness I found absent.

When we walked out of the arena,
the second before we scattered

to our SUVs, engines running heat,
any gawker could have marked

each member but not the starters,
not the studs. I could've been a Bear,

a Wolf, a Warrior, but I was a Star.
Over us, the sky filled with animals,

all but the brightest supergiants
lost in that anonymous chorus.

The world translates one way as a close shave
with teenage pregnancy. It translates as a car-
bomb, as cat litter that clumps for quick clean-up.
Why are we on the list for every chain letter?
Why does this itch? Why are you the walrus?
The world translates as a crude pictograph
scrawled in ink on the arm of our waitress.
We too have mapped the body and want a word
with the architect. We too swam the elementary
backstroke through the waters of high school,
repeating *chicken, airplane, jet; chicken,*
airplane, jet; and on and on until we grew out
of our clothes. The world translates, loosely,
as a constant attack on good family values.
Let's run down our checklist of necessities:
A healthy fear of sexually transmitted diseases?
Check. A desperate need to have our penises envied?
Check. We'll have you know we sleep
in the nude. We sleep like we mean it. We give
110% to sleep. So what about the world?
Personally, we preferred the world's Blue Period.
Personally, we thought we had one timeout left.
Hold still, the doctor told us. This will only hurt
forever. Then thankfully, it will all be over.

RANDY BE DROWNING

Reconstruct the reef—the staghorn,
bottlebrush, cat's paw, cluster coral—

and the subaquatic glow the moon
coaxed from the latticework undergirding.

For a single honors-elective credit,
we flippered through it, one-off cameras

dangling from our wrists, our breath
constricted to the nickel-width lifelines

of our snorkels. In my floating stasis,
I didn't think of how easily

some smartass could plug the tube,
ignored the ease at which my air

could be cut off, but not
Randy, who scooted off the transom

of the trawler and couldn't kick enough
to keep his head above the waves.

Randy be drowning, we ribbed him
after they back-slapped the water

from his lungs, the coughing stopped.
It became our refrain: *Randy be drowning*

when he blanked one minute
deep into his demonstration speech,

Randy be drowning when his safety school
said *nah*, when he surfaced lit

and barely present for the last exam.
An unplanned kid later, post-shift,

three Coors gone on his balcony,
he offered meth and needed me

to take it, a communion, an initiation
into his religion of letting go.

A quick *no*, and the gulf
widened, he floated farther away

and bobbed under, past the reef,
the sibilant Atlantic flux, the foam.

A silence unfolded, a shoal
of bluehead wrasse scouting the bubbles

beading from his mouth
that showed his savior where to dive.

FOR DENNIS, THE BLUE WHALE
I ADOPTED IN GRADE SCHOOL

Though it's years since I hoarded quarters,
licked letters closed for you, you're floating

along a sea ridge, stress lines pruning your skin.
Marking this year with more barnacles

in the deep, kettleblack ocean, you bellow out
your foghorn moans because you miss me

or my money, or what my money meant.
If Britannica's correct, you're only

middle-aged, have years to factor in a parable
or Bible verse with your ten-foot penis

and heart the size of a small golf cart.
When I can't sleep, I listen to your calling,

that deep, repetitive, meditative aid.
For all I know, you could be screaming.

silencer • 1. how it eats, taking in plankton, water, fish, expelling what doesn't stick to the plates in its mouth, how it travels no faster than a sedan through a school zone, how it can hold its breath for an hour, its throat the width of its bellybutton, its tongue as heavy as an elephant, its aorta wide enough for divers to float through, how it vocalizes in a low moan we can't hear, it sounds, they say, like singing, it sings for every reason, for mates, for warning, in loneliness, to test distances along the bottom of the sea, the death of its song could be a rock wall or the hull of a ship, how it might experience emotions, how it might feel things, how an animal doesn't always act like an animal—one nudged the shoulders of each diver who freed it from the crab trap lines when a flick of its tail could've crushed their puny bodies—the loudest animal on the planet, it passes at the speed of a commuter train rolling through an intersection, calling in a frequency we can't hear.

LIFEGUARD

Asterisk on the blacktop: dead crow
the camp van rolled over,

killed twice. He lies on the edge
of the dock. A rim around the lake

from lack of rain. Belly-up
canoe-pair beached

in the cutgrass and striped bass
trolling the muck-bed.

He drags a hand in
the narrows over

the dock-side, cutting the water
the boy breathes in,

the lake smooth-faced and silent.
Redwings dive for flies

as the water rushes
to reconstitute as glass, the lake

agitated from receiving
so many bodies.

He won't see the boy
lost against the flash

of pink one-pieces and orange
pool tubes—

pollen motes caught
in the afternoon's glow,

mosquito pinching his arm
as he watches the water,

stunned by the boredom of children
not drowning.

MY QUARRY

was ghastly vast, a throat too swollen
to swallow, as I followed you in—
you who owned a switchblade
and told me take it out only
if you're ready to use it.
You who toed the water naked
and lit a cigarette before dipping in.
My quarry, it dragged like a hook,
veiled you in the wreck
of a dredger for me to find.
We fell into atrophy
and used it as excuse
for what our hands were doing.
Me, unbelieving, weak from the jeans
I slipped off and tossed to an evergreen.
My back bone-white and bruised,
I wanted to be new for you.
You who chewed chaw, who swore
you'd pull me into a bar fight
some day. When you said
each year a bunch of teens
died in quarries I understood
before the beam of the night patrol
flashed the waves we hid below—
shaky ghost of a man I didn't know
and you a handhold away.

IMPROVISING

You, yes, you, the second wing steadying
the body. A steering aft paddle at the stern.

We stretch language
in our double bed you transform

into a boat, so I mime an oar and row.
You pull a quarter from my ear.

I pull a dove from your pillowcase.
You remove a flame you hid

in your throat, and I snip off my thumb.
It becomes an inchworm.

We are locked in the conceit,
I say. You say, We must be

prepared to go where the story goes.
You promise you can cut me in half

then reattach. You say the night
sets its bead on me, and you're the bolt

sparking fire in the underbrush.
I say I'm stone but no stone is skin

and no skin is stronger than your arrow.
So I'll earn a PhD in art history to learn

the right way to speak of beauty.
When I fail to bait the hook, you'll push

a night crawler through the barb.
When I need singles, you'll find change

in the collection plate. The point of this
is to make your partner look good.

My first mistake: morphing into a whale,
thinking a creature so large and brainless

couldn't register minor disruptions.
You tell me about a whale who kept her calf

in her mouth for days after it had died,
surfacing so it could breathe.

We are building this, I say, on sand. You say,
It grants us priceless views of the ocean.

THE NEXT GREAT AMERICAN ELEGY
IN THE EFFIGY OF

you, who bonged from a severed boar's head
Yuengling poured down its throat into your throat,
who let the jaws of that giant clamp yours in a kiss,
you, feral and triumphant in owning an animal for sport.
The initiation, every lowlife alky of the rugby team
opened their arms to welcome you in, you
who recoiled and took me to the road, thumbed a ride
in a pickup's bed, racing the interstate, us huddled
against the cab's back, first, speed a thrill
then our worry at its wildness. We matched
to the beast in us the engine's thrumming loop,
closed and continual, held in our mouths the tang
of blood, took our turns with the knife, rubber cut
from our One Star knockoffs, to have something
to cut. Bushwhacking through the American mythic,
we blunted, we blew by night-shift gas station
beauties who wove braids of gum in boredom
around their fingers. In the snowfall, the cooling
one long crescendo. We pissed on pole barns watched
by every animal the sky spread in its tapestry above us
and filled our bellies with meat-and-threes in Macon.
Put in off a back highway in Appalachia, we tubed
a river that carried us deep into the verdant country.
Our naked chests and unsaid desire to break
under the current, to cast our bodies to rapids,
the gift of that casting against all the pain that lay
in waiting, certain as the metronome

of a truck backing up. You, the dead king.
And in that reckoning, I beat my body to spare God
the task. A patch of your flannel caught
in the barb's bend, a pile of field rock we cleared
one summer to buy a beater—they low me, those rocks
descended from the firmament to the runnels
in the dirt. You had an eye for picking which to open,
which to split to dual crowns, galaxy of jewels
in the innards, an all-consuming purple bounty.

BREAKWATER

Egyptian lit has no myth
for this
struggle of muscle,

his fall off the break wall,
so I turn him fish—

my Aquaman
who had me

trace his body in chalk
on the walk outside the quad
after sectionals,

who bummed the keys
to my beater—

his Impala
impounded.

What a rush
that danger was
for him,

or must have been,

the moon hiding
behind stalks
of elm,

those dark witches
whispering *dive in.*

Did he watch
the waves a minute

before slipping
from his letterman,

the frost
accumulating lace
on the windshield?

Or, determined,
did he get in quickly?

In my telling, he takes
the form
of a blue whale
in the inky dark—

no crew cut, no
sharp smell of chlorine
in his hair,

he's mottled,
sulfur-bottomed, the boy
with fins.

But I keep seeing
his face in every face
I keep seeing. His face.

No, my boy doesn't perish

but breathes in a lake
the shape my hand made
in housepaint

on the back pocket
of his sweatpants.

That day, on break,
we lay in the bed
of the boss's pickup

before we taped
another wall off,

before he begged
the afternoon off,

before he took off in my boat
of an Oldsmobile
toward a lake the shape
of my open hand.

Some mornings I trace
the road to the cove.

The nets I keep
hauling up empty,

only half-hoping
for the fairy tale.

It's not the end, he told me once.
It's just the beginning
of the end.

sight • 1. red dots, chicken pox, roseola, / call to mind a pinch / of dye loosed in the water, blood / in the water, blood / on the sleeve, in the slip, / red dots of buckshot, back / acne the body manifests / in anger, red dot: the dog's right eye half-caught / by the spotlight, / or him / flashed in the image, red dots palmed / into the eye's periphery, / red where the gun touches, / the bullet leaves, / red-capped, torch at the match tip, the tip / of the bullet, the bull's-eye, / kill switch: erase / an insurgent by pressing it, / red dot on the forehead, point of a nerve, an adornment, / the perfect round, / to call a drive-by decorating the body, / a wound, preparing for a funeral, / red dot on a forehead, cycloptic, / red dot for distance, / laser tracer / that betrays the bullet's line, / red dot on the forehead, / red dot to tell / the bullet what's about / to unbecome.

AQUAMAN THINKS OF HIS YOUTH

First, the webs between his fingers found him
on the wrong side, then it was the scales

running up his arms. Then the unitard
his mother sewed. But he could swim and that

saved him, he could float like oil.
Every noon hour in the locker room

he put on lycra before the rest banged
through the door and began windmilling

towels. How long could he keep all this
hidden? His concave chest, his legs

fluttering through the pool, his ears buried
in the water's roar. When he pulled out

ahead of the rest and took the medal, a chain
around his neck, no one cared he dressed

in the dark, that he kept his bedroom door
locked and slipped out to the lake alone.

In the days before the green skin, the gills
like grill marks along his throat, the cutting,

his arms ticked in crosses. The jig up, the lake
a lure, a large target he squared himself to.

BLACK STRING OF DAYS

All night at Main Street, my polo shirt
orange with grease and red sauce,

I talked him down and tossed pan crust
when all he wanted was to take off

my pants, and all I wanted was a fishbowl
of Guinness and to finish

with my shift. A shared smoke
on the dumpster, stars glowing

like shotgun beads, he saved his gum
on his fingertip and left the ghost

of his ass in flour
on the plastic lid. To quit this,

to forfeit—I said, maybe you should
think about what they would do

with your dachshund, your fridge full
of condiments and milk. Think about

your mother and your mother's
boyfriend. Think even of me.

In the dark, the breakwater
called to him, called to him: *Come.*

DROWNING DOESN'T LOOK LIKE DROWNING

in the ward, it's deceptively quiet: a last
gasp, draining of color, a hand that travels

the valley between the bed and the body.
Waiting for something to happen, I see

the wound, again, open in the water
to swallow him. Is it that the lungs

fill with water when we go under?
No. The larynx, trying to protect itself,

kills us, closes up. He does nothing
but lie there, fed by a highway of tubes,

a cloverleaf interchange, all of it running
into him, the silver vein drawing up his arm

to the point of the lance. I want back in
the world I know. Because skin needs a cut

before it can heal, let him hammer me
with the dark's cool machinery—

the unknowable, what works
against the body—into that rendering.

KAI

Your name in Japanese is *ocean, shell,
recovery*. In Greek, it's *and*.

Out past the cutgrass, flatcars
slog through Minnesota's ghost herds,

tripping crossing lights in St. Cloud,
Fergus Falls, Grand Forks, south
where the desperate walk two miles—

Sacred Heart in Pine Ridge
to Stateline Liquor for a sixer.

I see your small figure backlit
on the plains. Fire in the Badlands,
shacks in the hills abandoned.

A bridge gives out as the second half
of a train rolls over it, and the front
heaves backward. No one

can get close enough, past the heat-wall,
to stop its burning.
Not even you, Ocean.

Stuck in the switching yard's sick
orange light, you wait without water
for two days, licking

the cold metal in the morning
for something wet.

I am calling *and*, I am chasing down
the ocean in your name. The city

comes out of fog in startling wholeness.
You curl into the hull of the seawall,

the water's clamorous voice
and the waves' white lacing.

When I call you, I plead *and and and.*

The train's wheels spin as fast
as buzz saws. Whatever you say,

you are fire. I wait through the night.
The stars wander toward their erasure.

BLOOD WORK

All night some critter roots gold teeth
from the shrubbery, phalanx
of uncut corn covers the field
in waves, and the rain barrel duplicates
the moon's white face, mold growth
in standing water. You wake to pain
registered in every limb's synapse,
each lit terminal, which I can do
nothing against and tell you so.
My St. Francis of the Wild,
of the Cloak of Birds chunked full
with an enema. I chain the pasture gate
although the horse is gone.
If the stars punch holes in the dark . . .
If I could hide you in my quiver . . .
Because I can't, I practice forgetting
providing against the question of heaven.
The dead call across the gap but go silent.
Because I can't, I play the mad king
torching the orchard before the blight
as they search the cell's inheritance,
and come back with the same story
in every retelling. Night watch,
night work, knitting the skin works
in the cut, what lays waiting in the cut.
My gasolined Daphne burns,
the peaches wrinkle in the heat, falling
from the tree limbs, the contrast liquid

runs fractured through the body's
endless hallways. My man feeds
a wolf with his viscera and reads the pills
by touch, their stamped indents.
He indexes the records and wakes late
to the evacuation of ants
from every pore of his skin.
Lying there, he lets them leave.
A whole colony that to raise his arms
he must convince a million tiny pieces
of himself to move, excite the particles
into shifting. Beyond the window,
evergreens like steeples sit watch
in the middle distance. My wolf
places his cry among the elements.
My wolf spreads grief through song
believing grief finite and transferrable—
an evil done of hunger and thus forgivable.

THE HURT SONNET

Dark days when I awaken so I slump
back to the swamp of his armpit, a whit
from the arachnid he inked to the stump
that's left. So close to the vestige of it,
the danger he's a reliquary of:
tattooed noose to venerate the fist
of a slug buried still in his back above
a white cross for the men he didn't miss.

If only I could strip off the black map
I sleep against and be his liniment,
gloss over the explosion, the mishap
phantom he feels in a forearm itch.

He won't leave the long tale his tattoos read
for me, so I'll amend the story.

ECHO

Breathless, then breathing—him out

of the water, the flames of waves—

he shivers off shivers like a coat—one sock on

then another—steps back from the pier—

backward through the hole

in the chain link—the late sun rising red

as a left-on burner—no answer—he calls out

against the silence—starts the Cutlass—

his trace—the skids in twin ribbons erase—

on the highway he hits sixty—almost home—

in reverse—

$\qquad\qquad\qquad\qquad\qquad\qquad$—reversed

$\qquad\qquad$ from home—almost hitting sixty on the highway—

$\qquad\qquad\qquad\qquad$ he leaves skids, twin ribbons traced to the lake

$\qquad\qquad\qquad\qquad\qquad\qquad$ where he killed the Cutlass for silence—

his burner left on—I called—no answer—

sun laced by the chain link—

he blows through the hole—one sock off

then another—shivers off shivers, then his coat—

on the pier, he eyes the waves of flame—him

in—breathing, then breathless

stock • 1. a shackle, bolt of wood, a billet, / the stump, what's
whittled down to / forearm size & fitted / to a barrel, a trigger, a
trigger / lock, called *furniture*, called kindling, / root fuel, what
comes / standard, the stock / model, what steadies the shot, / holds
the aim, what makes / a base, what some logger felled / to turn this
to This, the finish stripped / from cheek oil & holding, what / we
hurt by holding it not / doing anything with it but the having it /
in our hands, we hurt it, / it hurts us & who / we hold it to, / the
pedigree, the valuation, to keep / a supply of, everything carried,
every encumbrance, / what grounds the gun, what gives / footing
to the tree, in pieces: the fore-end / heel, toe, grip, thumbhole, /
not the teeth of the beast / but the backbone, / not the cut but
the knife on the tongue.

STRAY

She comes because I call her
and I've given her food,

which is to say I've kept her
alive. To form a bond

from such humble stuff she comes
when I call her, though

she's known violence
from hands like mine and from mine

when she clawed me
and I, in shock, sent her flying.

I had wanted to hold her
because she looked soft and hurt.

My father tells me
about a patient

who donated a kidney to her doctor
when his were failing

because the doctor had kept her
alive. I don't know why

I can't give of myself like that
for my father,

who is a doctor and certainly
saved the life of at least one person,

someone who wanted her life
saved, someone so grateful

she would repay him
with a kidney.

My father asks why I can't
give of myself like that.

The kitten asks only
for food, which I give her

so she'll come when I call her
and maybe, someday,

let me hold her.
As my father tells it,

the woman ended up
marrying the doctor,

so something like love,
or at least gratitude,

which can be a condition
of love, passed between them.

And a condition of faith,
which requires a sacrifice.

She knows the name I've offered
to her. She comes when called,

this creature so gentle and blameless
it costs me so little to save her.

AFTER DARK

I think of the deer that had run
across the road in the red glow of my braking
on other midnight drives,

as I crouch car-side on the gravel shoulder
with the heaving doe
bleeding out.

In these woods, I picked puffball mushrooms,
pinching from them small brown clouds.

Ones I left: raindrops touched off
their explosions, scattered their spores.

White face spotlit by my high beams.
In those seconds,

a frozen image of the doe drawn in the glass,
each ear turned its satellite toward me.

Long black eyelashes,
nostrils stirring up dervishes in the grit
of the shoulder.

All those herds I imagined sprinting
from the ditch's uncut switch grass to the line
of firs, the blackness beyond it. The night

stills. I'm the constant,
under a moon too big to be real.

THE PROBLEM WITH POETRY

The poem refused to wear shoes indoors, refused to stand
for the national anthem, refused elective surgery.
The poem refused rare steak and whole milk
and anything from the local grocer's freezer section.
Because he feared doctors, the poem refused medication,
experimental treatment, refused to sit down
when the doctor said, *Son, you better sit down.* The poem
came to my office hours after I had canceled class
to ask about his story. The poem brushed his teeth
with his index finger after waking in an unfamiliar bed
with an unfamiliar girl. The poem found religion.
The poem was a conscientious objector.
The poem carried a pistol pinched between his belt
and his button-up and fired it once at a stray dog.
The poem was a terrible shot. The poem wanted to be song.
The poem wanted to live like a river in the throat,
pouring out a world without end. The poem asked about
his story. The poem asked about the story he'd leave.

The front stone face lit by sun, the sides, black.
Magnolias shed petals to the netting
above the new grass. A photographer positions
a couple, pink buds as backdrop,
standing them center to hide the headstones.
We rest on the portico, legs free.
The sun falls on the hills behind us,
over memorials, a flock of wild turkeys—
grotesque shadows where they peck the grass
between the gravel paths. Cars in rows
along the crest, windows blank
in mirroring. The mausoleum is set
into the hillside so we walk
right onto the roof. From the Bay Bridge,
the glint of commuters coming home.
San Francisco somewhere behind the haze,
the varied shapes of downtown Oakland
only sketched in, a step toward the whole,
like finding a door by feeling the wall
around it. The caryatids are memories
of a sculptor's mold or a machine's
mindless whittling. Their arched backs,
their phantom hands. The hand stamp
you forgot to wash off from the dive bar
I mistake for a curling-iron burn. Dusk.
A light rain registers in the flood's beam.
A voice in the semi-dark: someone on the steps
of the bunker-like columbarium on his cell

standing at a distance that seems too far
for sound to travel. The city half-folded
in the valley turns on its small lights,
collecting as a swarm of bugs.
The night falls, and you struggle
to find the best way to make me
let go of myself, and I try to let go.

Lord, we'll sit out shivering because it's March.
We'll shiver but we'll sit out anyway. We'll talk.

Sitting here, we'll talk about how you made
the bumblebee, how you fitted on the wings,

breathed life into the bee and set the bee on stinging,
how you breathed life into me in that Nevada hotel.

You grabbed my mother's waist and blew. She grew
like a balloon. She got bigger as months went on

but never popped, never popped though she got
bigger as months went on, even the months that went

by faster. We'll sit here shivering because you made us
shiver to stay alive. You made the Bee Gees

to remind us we're alive. We've always
been alive. We're on our last life sitting here

after the sun has fallen but the sky is still light
and the cove is calling out its foghorn like a vacuum

running in an upstairs room. Lord, sit out front
with me. I'm freezing, but I've come to ask why

you quit us, why you ran out of breath—
you, my wind organ that only needed air

for music—why you left me to these mountains,
these mountains I'm sick of wanting. You knew

we'd get to this. You knew I'd serve cheap,
bottom-shelf whiskey, so I appreciate you coming.

We could sit here. We could breathe in air like smoke,
like smoke we'd breathe it in. We could sit here.

Always be closing the doors.

Always begin with the breath, breathe through the body's instinct to freeze.

Anyone seen the video of the Brazilian shooting?

Anyone seen the video of the Columbine shooting?

Anyone seen the video of the New Zealand shooting?

Anyone seen the video of the shooting at the farmers' market?
                    . . . the shooting at the salon?
                    . . . the shooting at the mosque?

Antecedent: what comes before what comes after.

Antecedent: what the pronoun erases.

Assess / Bolt / Counter

Assess. *When they yell get out*, the campus police officer told us, *get out.*

Barricade: flip tables, block the door.

Before and after: this is what the body looked like before, this is what it looks like now.

Bolt. *Be a survivor. Choose to be a survivor.*

Bulletproof backpacks are marketed to parents. One company boasts that their backpacks are "specially crafted to provide similar levels of protection as bulletproof vests" but with less conspicuous, fashion-forward design. They come in black, pink, and teal.

Call the police, then call your loved ones. *You can at least get in* goodbye.

Change is scary, change is an active threat.

Children with hands on their heads to signal they're not a part of the threat. Children with hands on their heads like sprinters at the end of the race, breathing heavily. Children looking like they're trying to keep their heads from floating away.

Counter. Chin him with the heel of your palm: *No one is going to fight for you if you don't fight for yourself.*

Clot the bleeding with a balled-up wad of paper.

Code red: whenever blood is leaving the body.

Colon: an interruption, a trigger for a list, a rundown. Two shots. A wavy grin of bullet holes still pocked in the siding at a Northwoods supper club from a raid during Prohibition. The novelty keeps the place in business because the food is garbage. The Thompson submachine gun mounted above the bar—for a tip, the bartender will take your pic with it, yoked like a lamb over your shoulders.

Comma: a pause, to make the sentence sensible.

Comma splice: what connects while it's severing.

Confetti: *Tear up paper to throw at The Shooter.* Maybe he'll be confused and think it's a party?

Deny your god.

Don't be afraid to get a little wild every once in a while.

Don't run in a straight line; trace Zs in the path of your running.

Don't run. *The police might mistake you for the threat.*

Don't just sit there and do nothing. Be the change you want to see in the world, and that change is stopping someone from shooting you and your classmates, your coworkers, your fellow concertgoers with a gun.

Doorstop: *Make a wedge with a rubberized sole.*

Ellipses identify the moments of absence, what the author excised. Three shots, three holes.

End-stops: to mark the stanzas that contain themselves.

Entropy: *Don't just sit there and do nothing. Don't let it happen* to *you.*

Evacuate / Evade / Engage

Fire alarms are often pulled to flood the halls with targets.

First, look for your exits, then leave.

Flyleaf: a blank page at the end of a book where there could be more story, but there isn't.

Full-stop: "a point beyond which it is impossible to proceed."

Generalities: we don't use his name, we bury him in the title The Shooter.

Get. Out.

God's on our side. We believe he's on our side.

Grab a textbook, they instructed my child, *and hug it to your chest over your heart.* My thickest textbook would have been the science reader. It contained an ark of animals, a transparent foldout of the body's musculature, and behind it, bones. It contained all the constellations in our galaxy, so if I held it to my chest, I would have been holding all that space, that vacuous distance, hoping a bullet couldn't rip through it.

Gun-shy: a slur hurled at those who handle guns like they handle hurt birds, or at a dog that startles at the report.

Hands hands hands.

Hands up: the signal for "I have a question." Or "I have an answer."

Hardening is necessary if you want to be the kind of person who makes it out.

He too believed that God was on his side. He believed that he was bringing them to their god, that he was serving the same role of an angel, a shepherd, the lamb yoked over his shoulders covered in blood.

Hebrew is read right to left, the end is where this sentence would begin.

Hiding as a survival strategy.

Hockey pucks as a survival strategy: *see* "For Defense Against Active Shooters, University Hands Out Hockey Pucks."

How can anyone write about flowers at a time like this? But I didn't mean *that* columbine, which blooms in the spring and isn't picky about where it grows as long as it's cared for.

I am a body, soft meat, made of numerous cabinet drawers where I could house a round.

If The Shooter believes that God is on his side, and if we believe that God is on our side, who is God listening to?

If someone acts, more people will survive.

"If you threw [a hockey puck] at a gunman, it would probably cause some injury. It would be a distraction, if nothing else."

In his mind, he was GOD, was god-warrior.

In the instance that he hits the other side of the office first, get out. The others will already be dead.

Just kidding. But everyone knows not to tell a joke about a gun in a school.

Knives? *Those are still fair game.*

Leave personal items behind.

Lock the doors. Lockdown.

Look out for yourself. The others will already be dead. Just kidding.

Make yourself small.

Never have anything in your hands, especially your phone. We might think you're holding a gun.

Old plan: shelter in place. New plan: get out. The others will already be dead.

Once, a student released a bunch of balloons on campus. When they hit tree branches, they popped, which tripped a lockdown. A crowd, gathered at a rally outside, quietly filed into the nearest offices, pushed metal cabinets to bar the doors. "What surprised me"—the featured speaker—"was how routine it all was, how calmly we evacuated the space."

Once, a theater professor tripped the alarm with a shot from a prop pistol. He wanted his students to see how fear really looked in each other's faces so that they could reenact that fear and make the audience believe in that fear.

One shot, and someone in the theater building called the police. A policeman entering the building got startled and fired a round into the ground next to his foot. A semi braking at the police lights backfired. A police car pulling a u-ie hit the curb and popped a tire. The consecutive *bangs* sent the students into a frenzy even though it was an empty threat, even though it started when a professor wanted to show his students what fear looked like in each other's faces.

Operational readiness—so that after a tragedy, a unit can get back to its regular day-to-day operations as soon as possible.

Options: *Bolt / Hide / Counter*

Parents are told not to come to the school.

Period, *informal*: "added to the end of a statement to indicate that no further discussion is possible or desirable," as in, "Do not come to the school, period."

Piggy pile on top of the individual. As if you've just won the championship on a buzzer-beater, the soccer tournament on a penalty, the swim meet on a sprint to the wall. As if you're the underdog who dropped the champ with a last-ditch haymaker.

Pronouns erase the naming of their referents—not the boy's name, not The Shooter, but *he*. In most cases, *he*. If we were thinking, we could wonder what's wrong with masculinity.

Punctuation: how to control the breathing, how to indicate when to breathe. Give your reader a chance to process before moving on. This could be a form of operational readiness if the tragedy is the sentence and what it says.

"[P]unctuation is cold notation; it is not frustrated speech; it is typographic code."

Punctuation: to mark with points or dots, how a clip full of bullets punctuates the body with periods, a series of full-stops.

Quiet your mind; breathe through the body's instinct to freeze.

Remember those semesters you carried a doorstop with you to class before you decided to recognize the fallacy of defense?

Run / Hide / Fight

Serifs are part of a letter's skeleton.

She Said Yes. Checked out from the rectory's library, I read it not as a model but a challenge and wondered why anyone would die over their faith when *no* is so easy to say.

Show me your hands, your hands. My hands are empty.

Silence your phone.

Spread out around the room so that The Shooter can't kill you all as quickly. If we spread out effectively, it will take longer for The

Shooter to kill all of us. We should practice how to spread out more effectively.

Stay down.

Syntax is a codified set of rules for determining relationships between clauses.

That's why he got so many kills. People didn't spread out.

The is the most frequently used word in the English language. We want everything to be so specific. It is not a gun, it is *the* gun. Someone once told me to take out every *the* from a poem. What a masculine impulse, he said, to make everything definite.

They didn't fight. That's why he got so many kills.

Throw staplers, rolls of tape, ripped pieces of paper, which—yes— won't hurt him but will distract him so that you can run toward him. That is, toward the man—in nearly all cases, a man, a white man— holding the weapon.

Tighten a belt around the door hinge. It might give you more time to spread out. It might slow down the rate at which you're all killed.

Two targets positioned side by side can look like a pair of wide eyes.

U: the shape of the iron sight above the forestock. I center the bead in it as I aim for a porcupine in the tree branches and shoot it down because my father told me it's a pest. I don't take a moment to consider his command. I shoot it, and it falls, knocking against the branches of the tree.

Violence. We are scared into our violences. Someone is coming to take something from us.

Why does God allow bad things to happen to good people? Does the fact this keeps happening to us prove that we are not, in fact, the good people?

With younger students, present it as a fire drill. Follow the leader, children. The building is burning, and we need to get out. If you all stay calm, children—we might say—you will not burn alive in this building, you will not have to watch your friends burn alive in front of you if you stay calm.

X marks the room where the shooting started.

X marks the spot of each kill.

X of arms, a child hugging her body.

X over the eyes of the dead in a children's cartoon.

Your co-workers—if you like them—you can warn them on your way out.

Your co-workers? You just need to be able to outrun the slowest one. Just kidding. But everyone knows not to tell a joke about a gun in a school.

Zigzag, trace Zs in the path of your running. Get a little wild every once in a while. *I can't stress this enough. I can't tell if you're listening. I can't tell you how to live if you're not.*

Zzzzzz: what we place in a bubble above the boy's head to show he's just sleeping.

NOTES

"My God" is after Sandra Beasley's poem of the same name and owes a debt to "The Foxhole Manifesto" by Jeffrey McDaniel.

"Black String of Days" borrows its title from a poem of the same name by Yusef Komunyakaa.

"How-To" was initially sparked by a mandated active-shooter training I attended, delivered by a member of the campus police at the university where I worked. The training's mnemonic—ABC for "assess," "bolt," "counter"—suggested the abecedarian form. An early draft of the poem ended with C. However, I couldn't escape the subject and kept returning to the draft until, eventually, it grew to consume the rest of the alphabet. Some of the italicized lines are taken nearly verbatim from the campus police officer, as recorded by my impromptu notetaking. Others are my best recollections of what was said.

The line "specially crafted to provide similar levels of protection as bulletproof vests" is taken from the ad copy for Bulletproof Zone's bulletproof bags and backpacks.

The line "a point beyond which it is impossible to proceed" is one of the definitions of "full-stop" given by the *Oxford English Dictionary*.

"For Defense Against Active Shooters, University Hands Out Hockey Pucks" is the title of an article published by NPR. The article reported on a plan by Oakland University, a public school that has a no-weapons policy, to distribute thousands of ninety-four-cent hockey pucks for personal defense. The text "If you threw [a hockey puck] at a gunman, it would probably cause some injury. It would be a distraction, if nothing else" is taken from that article.

The line "added to the end of a statement to indicate that no further discussion is possible or desirable" is one of the definitions of "period" from *OxfordLanguages*.

The line "[P]unctuation is cold notation; it is not frustrated speech; it is typographic code" is from Robert Bringhurst's *The Elements of Typographic Style*.

She Said Yes: The Unlikely Martyrdom of Cassie Bernall is the title of a book about one of the victims of the Columbine school shooting written by the mother of the victim. I first encountered the book, which was recommended to me by my church's youth-group coordinator, when I was in high school. A classmate of Bernall's who survived the shooting reported that in the Columbine library, Bernall refused to deny her faith after one of the shooters challenged her, at which point, in response, the shooter killed her. This led many in Christian circles to hold up Bernall as a martyr who lived her faith. According to later reporting in the *Washington Post*, the shooter had confronted a different student in the library about their faith but became distracted and moved away, and that student wasn't shot. The classmate who made the original report apparently confused Bernall and this other student. I did not know of this context when I first read *She Said Yes*.